PIGS
ON THE FAMILY FARM

Chana Stiefel

Enslow Elementary
an imprint of

Enslow Publishers, Inc.
40 Industrial Road
Box 398
Berkeley Heights, NJ 07922
USA
http://www.enslow.com

CONTENTS

WORDS TO KNOW

boar—A male pig.

breed—A kind of animal in a group.

lard—Pig fat.

piglet—A baby pig.

snout—A pig's nose.

sow—A female pig.

swine—Another name for pigs.

PARTS OF A PIG

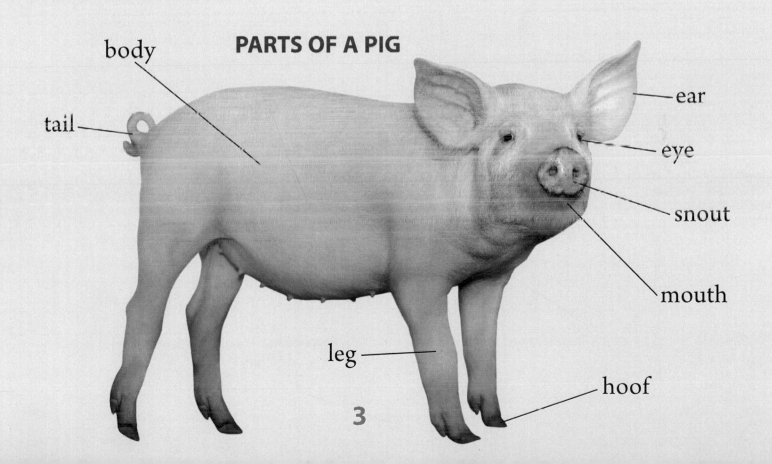

body

tail

ear

eye

snout

mouth

leg

hoof

PIGS **DIG**

4

Pigs have a great
sense of smell.

Did you know that a pig digs in the dirt with its **snout**? It sniffs for roots, acorns, and bugs to eat. Dig in for more fun facts about pigs on the family farm!

"OINK, OINK!"

Matt and Tara raise pigs on their family farm. They raise many other animals, too. Their children, Jack and Alice, lend a helping hand.

Matt and Tara raise eight adult pigs on their farm. Pigs are also called swine.

PIGGING
OUT

Most of the year, Matt and Tara's pigs wander in the fields. They eat roots, leaves, grass, weeds, and bugs. Matt and Tara also feed the pigs corn, wheat, barley, oats, and peas. The grain is soaked in milk. The mushy mixture is better for their bellies.

Matt feeds his pigs roasted soybeans and walnuts to snack on.

JUNK FOOD

In winter, Jack helps get the pigs into the barn. He brings a pail of compost. Compost is a mix of vegetable scraps, sour milk, yogurt, eggs, and eggshells. The pigs love the stinky smell. They follow Jack back to the barn. Then they eat a compost treat!

Pigs love to eat compost. Compost also helps plants grow in the garden when it is added to the soil.

The floor of the barn is covered with hay.

The larger male pig is on the left. The female is on the right.

BIG PIGS

Pigs can grow very large. On Matt and Tara's farm, a female pig can weigh as much as 400 pounds. A male may weigh about 700 pounds. A pig that weighs more than 120 pounds is called a hog.

LITTLE
PIGGIES

If a piglet gets sick, the farmer gives it herbs that heal. He may also keep it away from other pigs. He feeds the piglet simple foods and uses a heat lamp to keep it warm.

A baby pig is called a **piglet**.

Its father is called a **boar**.

Its mother is a **sow**.

The pigs grunt to each other.

This is how they "talk."

The pigs like to lie down close to each other when they sleep.

MESSY MUD
BATH

Pigs do not sweat. On hot days, pigs cool off by rolling in the mud. The mud also protects the pigs from bug bites and sunburn.

Pigs might look muddy sometimes, but they like to keep clean.

The family sells healthy food from their barn. Many people visit and buy what they need to eat.

PASS THE
BACON

Matt and Tara raise pigs for meat. Ham, bacon, pork, and sausage all come from pigs. The fat of a pig is called **lard**. Lard is used for cooking and baking. People come to the farm to buy fresh meat and lard.

MANY KINDS OF PIGS

Not all pigs are the same. There are many different **breeds**. A Yorkshire is one breed of pig. Which one do you like best?

KuneKune

Duroc

Yorkshire

Berkshire

Tamworth

LIFE CYCLE OF A PIG

1. A sow gives birth to 4 to 13 piglets at a tim[e]. She may have two litters a ye[ar].

2. The piglets drink milk from their mother. By one month, they start to eat grain.

3. Pigs are fully grown at 3 to 5 years old. Pigs may live for about 10 to 15 years.

LEARN MORE

BOOKS

Macken, JoAnn Early. *Pigs*. Pleasantville, N.Y.: Weekly Reader, 2010.

Mercer, Abbie. *Pigs on a Farm*. New York: PowerKids Press, 2010.

Minden, Cecilia. *Farm Animals: Pigs*. Ann Arbor, Mich.:
   Cherry Lake Publishing, 2010.

WEB SITES

Science Kids. *Animal Facts.* **"Fun Facts about Pigs."**
   http://www.sciencekids.co.nz/sciencefacts/animals/pig.html

Smithsonian National Zoological Park. *Kids' Farm.*
   http://www.nationalzoo.si.edu/Animals/KidsFarm/IntheBarn

INDEX

Enslow Elementary, an imprint of Enslow Publishers, Inc.
Enslow Elementary® is a registered trademark of Enslow Publishers, Inc.

Copyright © 2013 by Chana Stiefel

Library of Congress Cataloging-in-Publication Data
   Stiefel, Chana, 1968-
   Pigs on the family farm / Chana Stiefel.
      p. cm. — (Animals on the family farm)
   Summary: "An introduction to an animal's life on a farm for early readers. Find out what a pig eats, where it lives, and what pigs are like on a farm"—Provided by publisher.
   Includes index.
   ISBN 978-0-7660-4208-7
   1. Swine—Juvenile literature. I. Title. II. Series: Animals on the family farm.
   SF395.5.S74 2014
   636.4—dc23
                    2012028804

Future editions:
Paperback ISBN: 978-1-4644-0359-0
EPUB ISBN: 978-1-4645-1198-1
Single-User PDF ISBN: 978-1-4646-1198-8
Multi-User PDF ISBN: 978-0-7660-5830-9

Printed in the United States of America
012013 The HF Group, North Manchester, IN
10 9 8 7 6 5 4 3 2 1

To Our Readers: We have done our best to make sure all Internet Addresses in this book were active and appropriate when we went to press. However, the author and the publisher have no control over and assume no liability for the material available on those Internet sites or on other Web sites they may link to. Any comments or suggestions can be sent by e-mail to comments@enslow.com or to the address on the back cover.

Photo Credits: Howling Wolf Farm, pp. 6, 7, 9, 18; Julie Hunt Connel, p. 21 (left); National Swine Registry, p. 20 (right); Photos.com: Chris Hepburn, p. 21 (middle), Craig W. Walsh, p. 17, Harry Lines, p. 16, Imke Schulze, p. 22 (left), Ivonne Wierink-vanWetten, pp. 4–5, John Marquess, p. 14; Shutterstock.com, pp. 1, 2, 3, 8, 10, 11, 15, 19, 20 (left), 21 (right), 22 (right top, right bottom); © Wayne Hutchinson /FLPA/ Minden Pictures, p. 12.

Cover Photo: Simone van den Berg/Photos.com

A note from Matt and Tara of Howling Wolf Farm: Howling Wolf Farm grows vital food to feed individuals and families. Products include vegetables, dry beans and grains, dairy, beef, eggs, chicken, lamb, and pork. We work in partnership with nature and people to grow vibrant, abundant food. We farm with an intention of creating a farm and food to bring health, vitality, and enjoyment to our complete beings and the land. We focus on heirloom and open-pollinated varieties, heritage breeds, and wild foods.

Series Science Consultant:
Dana Palmer
Sr. Extension Associate/4-H Youth Outreach
Department of Animal Science
Cornell University
Ithaca, NY

Series Literacy Consultant:
Allan A. De Fina, Ph.D.
Past President of the New Jersey Reading
   Association
Dean of the College of Education
New Jersey City University
Jersey City, NJ